Predators
in the
Rain Forest

Saviour Pirotta

RSVP

RAINTREE
STECK-VAUGHN
PUBLISHERS
A Steck-Vaughn Company

Austin, Texas

Deep in the Rain Forest

PEOPLE in the Rain Forest

PREDATORS in the Rain Forest

RIVERS in the Rain Forest

TREES AND PLANTS in the Rain Forest

Cover picture: A spectacled cayman opens its jaws in the Amazon of Venezuela.

Title page: Two jaguars in South America

Contents page: A green tree boa in the Amazon, hanging from a tree

Published by Raintree Steck-Vaughn Publishers, an imprint of Steck-Vaughn Company

Printed in Italy. Bound in the United States.
1 2 3 4 5 6 7 8 9 0 03 02 01 00 99

Library of Congress Cataloging-in-Publication Data
Pirotta, Saviour.
Predators in the rain forest / Saviour Pirotta.
    p.   cm.—(Deep in the rain forest)
    Includes bibliographical references and index.
    Summary: Describes the different types of predatory animals that inhabit the rain forests of the world and discusses their habits, hunting methods, and survival techniques.
    ISBN 0-8172-5132-4 (hard); 0-8172-8113-4 (soft)
    1. Rain forest animals—Juvenile literature.
    2. Predatory animals—Juvenile literature.
    [1. Rain forest animals. 2. Predatory animals.]
    I. Title. II. Series.
    QL112.P56 1999
    591.734—dc21   98-4588

Contents

Rain Forests Around the World

Rain forests are thick forests in parts of the world where there is lots of rain. Most rain forests are near the equator, an imaginary line that runs around the center of the earth. The largest rain forest is the Amazon, in South America.

African fish ▶ eagles can spot fish far below them with their excellent eyesight.

Tigers live ▶ mainly in India and South Asia.

EQUATOR

▲ Chameleons live in southern India and Sri Lanka.

The rain forests are home to many predators. Predators are animals that kill other animals for food. They come in many sizes, from tiny centipedes to big tigers and jaguars.

◀ An eyelash viper in Costa Rica opens its jaws.

KEY

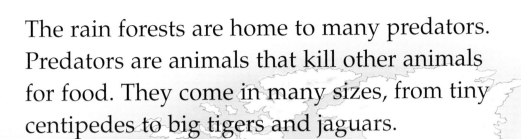 The green areas on the map show rain forests.

▲ A spectacled cayman in Venezuela

▲ The giant otter of Brazil is one of the world's rarest mammals.

On the Forest Floor

One of the smallest predators on the forest floor is the centipede. Some centipedes have jaws containing poison that kills their prey. One kind of centipede in Central America can kill a human with its bite.

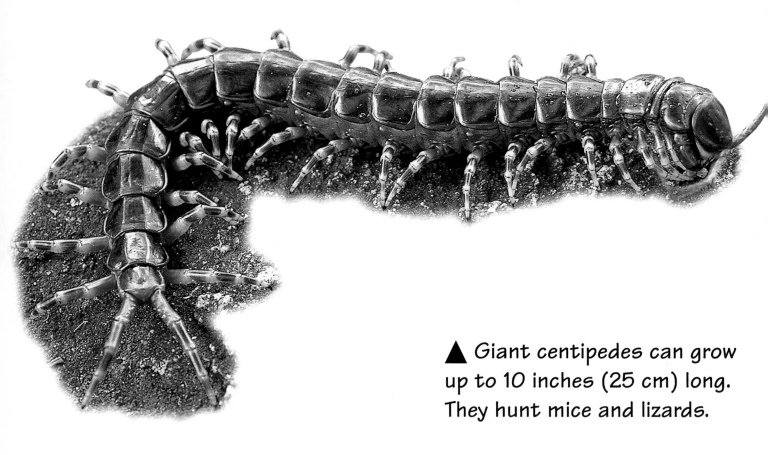

▲ Giant centipedes can grow up to 10 inches (25 cm) long. They hunt mice and lizards.

Rain forest scorpions like to hide under damp logs and leaves. Scorpions usually crush their prey to death, using their claws.

If bigger predators such as monkeys attack them, scorpions use the poison in the ends of their tails to defend themselves.

▲ Mother scorpions carry their young on their backs.

Spiders

Some spiders are also poisonous. They kill their prey by injecting poison through their fangs.

Tarantulas in the Amazon can kill moths, flies, and beetles with just one bite. The bird-eating spider is one of the largest spiders in the world. Its leg span is up to 7 inches (18 cm) wide.

▼ This hungry tarantula is eating a snake.

Trap-door spiders make silk-lined burrows underground. With moss or soil, they build a roof that opens like a trapdoor.

▲ A trap-door spider in Jamaica opening the door of its burrow

The spider sits in its burrow, waiting to feel the movement of birds or small animals passing by. Then it darts out of the door and pounces!

9

Big cats

The largest predators in the rain forest are the big cats. Jaguars live in Central and South America. They prey mainly on capybaras, wild pigs, and fish.

Tigers live mainly in India and southern Asia. They prey on wild pigs, deer, cattle, birds, and fish. But some can turn into man-eaters!

A tiger looking for fish ▶ in Sumatra, Indonesia

▼ Two jaguars snarl at each other over a resting place.

Jaguars have spotted coats, and tigers have striped coats. With this camouflage they can creep up on their prey unnoticed.

Jaguars and tigers are both excellent swimmers, and they catch fish with ease.

In the Trees

Most predators live high up in the trees. All the animals have to watch out for bigger predators who hunt them.

Chameleons are masters of surprise. They change the colors of their bodies to match their surroundings. Chameleons can grow up to 16 inches (40 cm) long and 5 inches (13 cm) high.

▲ Chameleons' tongues move at lightning speed to snatch their prey.

Some cats hunt in the trees. They have powerful claws to help them climb.

▲ A margay with a freshly caught rat, high up in a tree

The margay of South America is a climbing cat. It hunts mostly at night. Margays can chase mice and lizards right to the top of a tree. They kill with a powerful bite.

Camouflage

Many animals use camouflage to hide from predators. Green tree frogs have bright-green bodies, so it is hard to see them in a tree.

▼ Sticky pads on a tree frog's feet help it cling to leaves.

A leaf katydid in Costa Rica ▶

Leaf katydids also hide, using camouflage. Their bodies look exactly like leaves.

Poison arrow frogs are different. Their bright colors have a purpose. They warn any predators tempted to eat the frogs that they are poisonous.

▼ Blue poison arrow frogs in Brazil

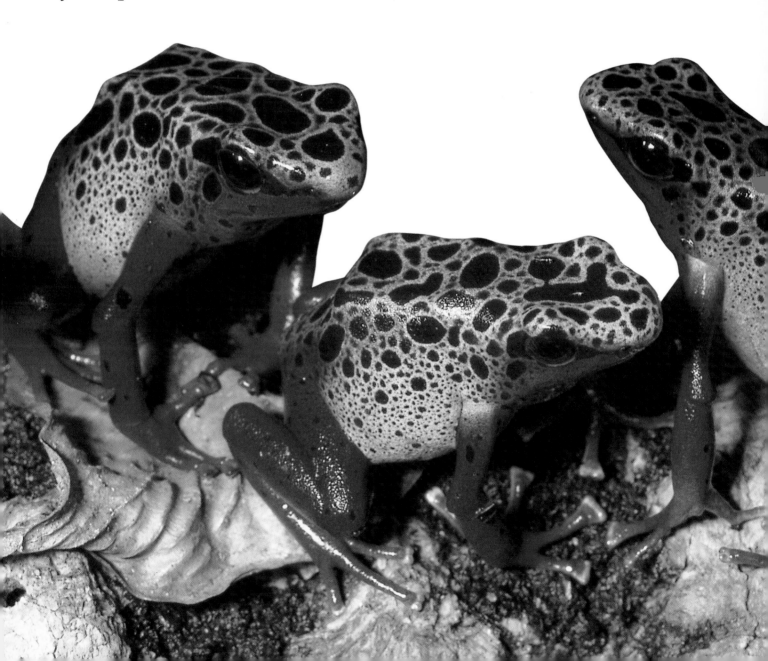

Snakes

There are over 160 different kinds of snakes in the rain forest. Some, like the anaconda, live along muddy riverbanks.

Coral snakes live under logs or stones on the forest floor. The green tree boa makes its home in the trees.

◀ The green tree boa looks just like its surroundings.

The biggest snake in the Amazon is the anaconda. It can grow up to 20 feet (6 m) long.

Anacondas lurk along riverbanks, waiting for their prey to come to the river to drink. They grab their victims and squeeze them to death. Then they swallow them whole.

▼ A hungry anaconda squeezes a cayman to death.

Poisonous fangs

Vipers are not as big as anacondas. They grow up to only 6 feet (2 m) long. But they are just as deadly. Vipers use fangs to kill their prey instead of squeezing them to death. Their fangs inject poison.

Many vipers have special pits between their eyes and their nostrils. These help them sense their prey in the dark.

▲ A hog-nosed viper swallows a large frog.

Vipers attack mostly small animals such as lizards. But some can kill people, too.

◀ The golden eyelash viper is deadly poisonous.

In the Sky

Eagles live in the highest part of the rain forest. They have one mate for life and build large nests in the tops of trees.

Eagles have excellent eyesight. As they glide above the canopy, they can spot the slightest movement in the greenery below.

Harpy eagles live ▶ in rain forests throughout the Amazon.

20

All eagles have razor-sharp talons to catch their prey. They use their sharp, hooked beaks to eat.

Crested serpent eagles eat snakes and lizards. They kill their prey by stamping on them.

An African fish eagle ▶ clutches a freshly caught fish in its sharp talons.

21

Rivers and Lakes

The lakes and rivers of the rain forest are full of hungry predators. The biggest are the crocodiles and caymans. When hunting, they float just under the surface of the water, with only their eyes and nostrils showing.

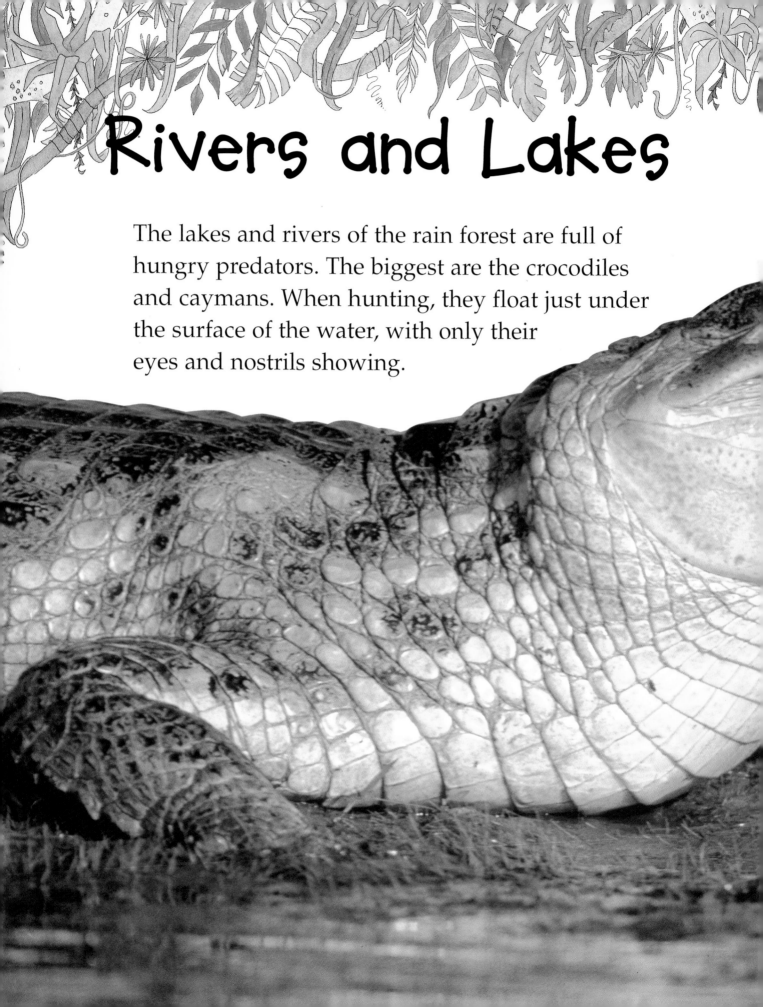

◀ A spectacled cayman has many teeth to catch and eat its food.

Crocodiles and caymans drag large animals underwater to drown. Smaller ones are gobbled up immediately.

A crocodile munches a snake ▶ in northern Australia.

23

Otters and eels

Electric eels in the Amazon River can grow up to 6 feet (2 m) long. They hunt by stunning fish with an electric jolt of up to 650 volts, which makes them easy to catch.

▼ An electric eel in South America

The giant otter is the largest otter in the world. Its tail and four webbed feet help it move quickly through the water, to catch small mammals and birds.

▼ A hungry otter eats a fish lunch.

Fierce fish

Piranhas are the fiercest fish in the Amazon. They swim in large schools. When they find prey, they tear it to pieces in a frenzy with their razor-sharp teeth.

▼ A school of piranhas in a feeding frenzy

Piranhas can make mincemeat of large animals. They can be deadly to people, too.

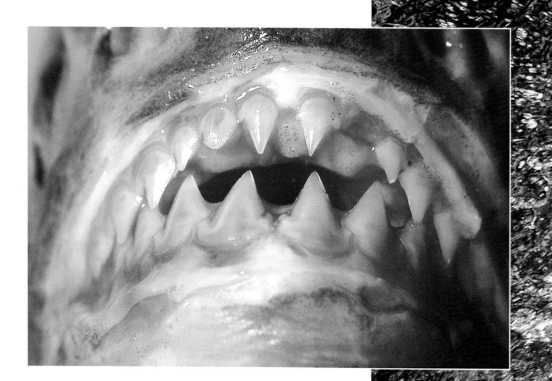

▲ Piranhas' teeth are so sharp that rain forest people sharpen their spears with them.

Stingrays are big, flat fish that bury themselves in the sand. The stingray has a long tail with a poisonous sting at the tip, which it uses to hunt small crabs and fish.

▲ A stingray pops up its eyes to look for food.

27

Crocodile Mask

Make your own crocodile jaws by following the instructions below.

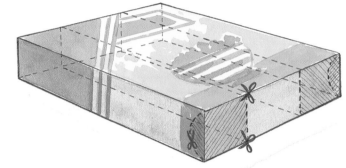

1. Cut off the sides of a cereal box. With each piece, cut off one end and cut out a semicircle. Cover the two pieces with brown paper, so they are easier to paint later.

Ask an adult to help you fasten the two jaws together with paper fasteners. Push the fasteners through from the inside to the outside.

3. Stick the foil onto the poster board strips, using glue. Then cut out six strips of teeth.

4. Attach the teeth to the jaws with tape.

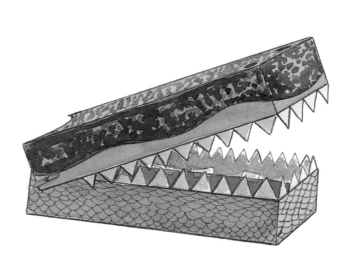

5. Paint scales and speckles on the jaws. Paint the inside of the mouth red. Don't forget to add the nostrils!

6. Make a hole on each side of the top jaw and thread elastic through. Tie the elastic so it can go around the back of your head and hold your crocodile jaws on.

Glossary

Amazon A region of rain forest in South America around the Amazon River.

Burrows Underground homes of animals.

Cayman A type of alligator, which lives in South America.

Camouflage Color and shape that disguises creatures so they look like their surroundings.

Katydid A type of grasshopper.

Leg span The widest measurement between a spider's legs.

Margay A small, wild cat with a dark-striped coat. It can only be found in South and Central America.

Predators Creatures that kill others for food.

Prey Creatures that are killed by others for food.

Trapdoor A door or hatch in a roof or floor.

Viper A type of poisonous snake.

Webbed feet Feet that are connected by a membrane of skin. They help an animal swim faster by acting like flippers.

Further Information

Other books to read

Cherry, Lynne. *The Great Kapok Tree: A Tale of the Amazon Rain Forest*. San Diego: Harcourt, Brace, Jovanovich, 1990.

Grupper, Jonathon. *Destination—Rain Forest: Rain Forest*. Washington, DC: National Geographic, 1997.

Harris, Nicholas. *Into the Rainforest: One Book Makes Hundreds of Pictures of Rainforest Life* (The Ecosystems Xplorer). Alexandria, VA: Time Life, 1996.

Lewington, Anna. *Atlas of the Rain Forests*. Austin, TX: Raintree Steck-Vaughn, 1997.

Nagda, Ann Whitehead. *Canopy Crossing: A Story of an Atlantic Rainforest*. Norwalk, CT: Soundprints Digital Audio, 1997.

Osborne, Mary Pope. *Afternoon on the Amazon*. (First Stepping Stone Books). New York: Random House, 1995.

CD Rom

Exploring Land Habitats (Raintree Steck-Vaughn, 1997)

Useful addresses

All these groups provide material on rain forests for schools:

Earth Living Foundation
P.O. Box 188
Hesperus, CO 81326
(970) 385-5500

Friends of the Earth
1025 Vermont Avenue NW
Suite 300
Washington, D.C. 20005-6303
(202) 783-7400

Reforest the Earth
2218 Blossomwood Court NW
Olympia, WA 98502

The World Rainforest Movement
Chapel Row
Chadlington
Oxfordshire OX7 3NA
Tel: 01608 676691

World Wildlife Fund
1250 24th Street NW
P.O. Box 96555
Washington, D.C. 20077-7795

Picture acknowledgments
Bruce Coleman *title page, contents page* , 10–11 (Luiz Claudio Marigo), 10 (bottom) (Alain Compost), 15 (top) (Michael Fogden), 15 (bottom) (Rod Williams), 16 (Luiz Claudio Marigo), 19 (John Cancalosi); Getty Images *Cover* (Art Wolfe), 22–23 (Schafer & Hill); Image Bank 14 (James Carmichael); NHPA 6 (Stephen Dalton), 12 (Norbert Wu), 17 (Martin Wendler), 21 (E.A.James), 24 (Robert Wu); Oxford Scientific Films 7 (Phil Devries), 8 (Nick Gordon), 9 (J.A.L.Cooke), 13 (Partidge Films Ltd), 18 (Michael Fogden), 23 (David Curl), 26 (Jany Sauvanet), 26–27 (Sean O'Driscoll), 27 (Max Gibbs); Still Pictures 20 (Daniel Heuclin), 25 (Nicole Duplaix). Border and folio artwork: Kate Parsons. Map pages 4–5: Peter Bull.

Index

Page numbers in **bold** show there are pictures on the page as well as information.